WHAT ARE MICROAGGRESSIONS?

By Meghan Green

Published in 2023 by
KidHaven Publishing, an Imprint of Greenhaven Publishing, LLC
29 East 21st Street
New York, NY 10010

Copyright © 2023 KidHaven Publishing, an Imprint of Greenhaven Publishing, LLC.

All rights reserved. No part of this book may be reproduced in any form without permission in writing from the publisher, except by a reviewer.

Designer: Andrea Davison-Bartolotta
Editor: Jennifer Lombardo

Photo credits: Cover (top) chairoij/Shutterstock.com; cover (bottom) Dmytro Zinkevych/Shutterstock.com; p. 5 Everett Collection/Shutterstock.com; p. 7 fizkes/Shutterstock.com; p. 9 Monkey Business Images/Shutterstock.com; p. 11 RONNACHAIPARK/Shutterstock.com; p. 13 Prostock-studio/Shutterstock.com; p. 15 (top) BBSTUDIOPHOTO/Shutterstock.com; p. 15 (bottom) Gorodenkoff/Shutterstock.com; p. 17 (main) wavebreakmedia/Shutterstock.com; p. 17 (inset) limpido/Shutterstock.com; p. 19 michaela0990/Shutterstock.com; p. 21 iunewind/Shutterstock.com.

Library of Congress Cataloging-in-Publication Data

Names: Green, Meghan, author.
Title: What are microaggressions? / Meghan Green.
Description: New York, NY : KidHaven Publishing, [2023] | Series: What's
  the issue? | Includes bibliographical references and index.
Identifiers: LCCN 2022010043 | ISBN 9781534542112 (library binding) | ISBN
  9781534542099 (paperback) | ISBN 9781534542105 (set) | ISBN
  9781534542129 (ebook)
Subjects: LCSH: Microaggressions–Juvenile literature. |
  Prejudices–Juvenile literature. | Discrimination–Juvenile literature.
Classification: LCC HM1091 .G74 2023 | DDC 303.3/85–dc23/eng/20220301
LC record available at https://lccn.loc.gov/2022010043

Printed in the United States of America

Some of the images in this book illustrate individuals who are models. The depictions do not imply actual situations or events.

CPSIA compliance information: Batch #CSKH23: For further information contact Greenhaven Publishing LLC, New York, New York at 1-844-317-7404.

Please visit our website, www.greenhavenpublishing.com. For a free color catalog of all our high-quality books, call toll free 1-844-317-7404 or fax 1-844-317-7405.

CONTENTS

Breaking Down the Word	4
Aimed at Certain Groups	6
Racial Prejudice	8
Prejudice Against LGBTQ+ People	10
People with Disabilities	12
Prejudice Against Women	14
Why Do Microaggressions Hurt?	16
Listening and Learning	18
How to Handle Microaggressions	20
Glossary	22
For More Information	23
Index	24

Breaking Down the Word

What exactly is a microaggression? Let's start by looking at the parts of the word. "Micro" is a word that means small. "Aggression" means acting angrily toward another person, often without any real reason. When we talk about microaggressions, we're talking about small comments or actions that show **prejudice** against a certain group.

A microaggression may be small, but it can have big results. When someone deals with a lot of microaggressions every day, they can feel like these comments or actions are piling up. This makes the person feel worse.

Facing the Facts

A doctor named Chester M. Pierce came up with the word "microaggression" in the 1970s.

The opposite of micro is macro. The U.S. **segregation** laws were an example of a macroaggression against Black people.

5

Aimed at Certain Groups

Some people think microaggressions aren't real. They say people are too **sensitive** and should just ignore mean comments. However, microaggressions are about more than being mean. They're words or actions that show a person's prejudice against those in groups that are already **discriminated** against.

People of color, people in the **LGBTQ+ community**, people with disabilities, women, and those in other groups often have to deal with microaggressions. Most of the time, a person who's responsible for a microaggression isn't trying to be mean. However, their words or actions still hurt people.

Facing the Facts

Some people say that "impact matters more than intent." This means how your words and actions make someone feel matters more than what you meant by them.

People may face microaggressions related to their religion, or belief system.

7

Racial Prejudice

Racism, or prejudice against people of color, is a problem in the United States and other parts of the world. People of color face microaggressions very often because other people—especially white people—tend to have certain ideas about people of other races that aren't always true.

One example of a racial microaggression is when an Asian person who was born and raised in the United States is told that their English is very good. This sounds like a nice thing to say, but it sends the message that the speaker thinks the Asian person doesn't really belong in the United States.

Facing the Facts

According to a study, Black adults are the group that is most likely to report experiencing microaggressions. Black men are more than twice as likely as Black women to say that others act as if they're afraid of them.

Asking an American person of color what country they "really" come from is a microaggression.

Prejudice Against LGBTQ+ People

Another group that often deals with microaggressions is the LGBTQ+ community. Sometimes these come from outside the community. For example, a person who is cisgender, meaning the gender they were assigned at birth, might use the wrong name or pronouns for a **transgender** person.

Other times, the microaggressions may come from within the community. For instance, people who are **asexual** may hear from other LGBTQ+ people that they don't belong in the community. This sometimes happens to people in other groups too. Hearing this from other people who know what it feels like to be discriminated against can be very upsetting.

Nearly all people who are part of the LGBTQ+ community face microaggressions at one time or another.

Facing the Facts

One of the biggest microaggressions people in the LGBTQ+ community face is the suggestion that they're not normal or they can change their identity, or sense of self. These suggestions aren't true or fair to LGBTQ+ people.

11

People with Disabilities

There are many kinds of disabilities. Some are easy to see, such as when a person is missing a body part. Other disabilities are invisible. They can't be seen on the outside. For example, heart problems are invisible, but they can make it much harder for people to walk long distances.

Telling someone they "look fine" and must not really need a wheelchair or cane to walk is one example of a microaggression. Another is overlooking the **accommodations** a disabled person needs. This means many disabled people can't take part in certain activities.

Facing the Facts

The word for prejudice and discrimination against people with disabilities is "ableism."

Making a joke about a person's wheelchair is a microaggression.

Prejudice Against Women

For many years, women didn't have the same rights as men. Today, women still have to fight to be taken seriously, especially in the workplace. One microaggression that women often deal with is being told to smile more.

Like most microaggressions, this might not seem like a big deal, but it sends a bigger message. Women are told to smile because people think it makes them look more pleasant. Women who choose not to smile are often seen as rude. Most men don't have to deal with people trying to control their behavior this way.

Facing the Facts

Black women face microaggressions about both their race and their gender. Understanding that someone can face more than one kind of discrimination at a time is called intersectionality.

Some people still think women aren't as good as men at some jobs, even when they've been doing them for years.

15

Why Do Microaggressions Hurt?

Most people don't mean to hurt others. They often think their microaggressions are **compliments** or jokes. However, what we need to remember about microaggressions is that many people hear them all the time.

Imagine that you don't like your haircut. You're not upset at first because you know it'll grow out. Your mom makes a joke about it, and you laugh. Later, your teacher says something about it. All your classmates make a joke or a comment. By this time, you're starting to feel really badly about your hair. A microaggression feels worse because it's about something a person can't change, unlike a haircut.

Facing the Facts

Microaggressions don't just hurt a person's feelings. Because they're attacks on who a person is, they can cause major health problems, such as **depression**.

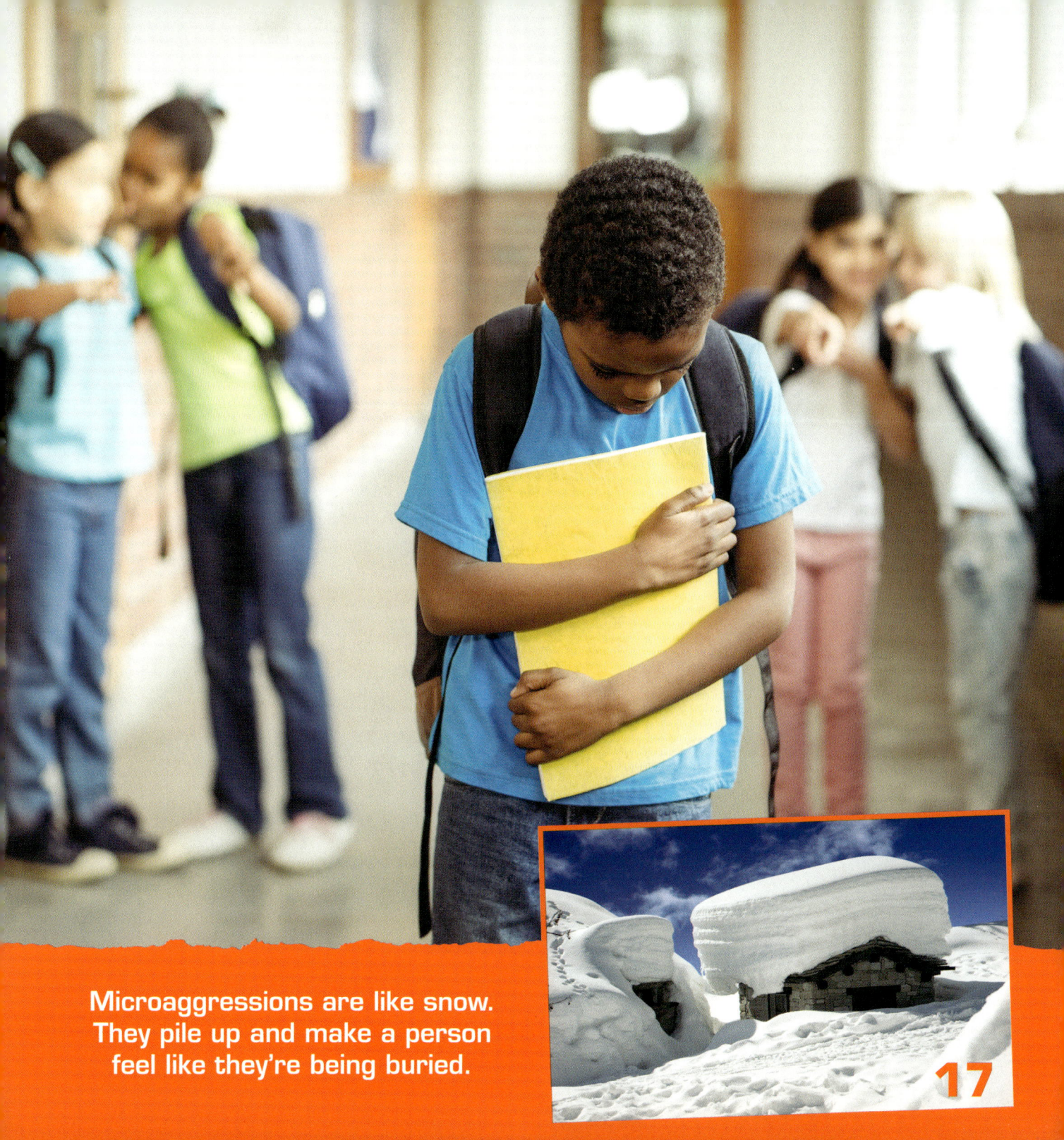

Microaggressions are like snow. They pile up and make a person feel like they're being buried.

17

Listening and Learning

Another big reason why microaggressions are hurtful is because they can **invalidate** people. They sometimes show that the person committing the microaggression isn't really interested in getting to know the other person. Instead, they're just coming up with a false idea of what that person is like based on **stereotypes**.

You can help by listening to people when they tell you something is hurtful. Try to understand why they're saying that. Don't just tell them you didn't mean to hurt them. Pay attention to the things you notice about people and think about why you notice those things.

Facing the Facts

Experts say microaggressions happen when our brains get "stuck" on someone's differences. The harder we try to ignore them, the more we focus on them.

Steps to Avoid Microaggressions

Pay attention to what you notice. — When you first meet someone, notice what things about them jump out at you.

Question yourself. — Later, think about what you noticed. What thoughts did you have about those things? Why do you think you had those thoughts?

Understand that it's not just you. — Think about the ways your friends, parents, school, TV shows, and others have **reinforced** the stereotypes you believe.

Don't pretend you don't notice. — Some people pretend they don't see people's differences, but the truth is that we all do. What matters is how we act toward people who are different from us.

Listen, and believe people. — Believe people when they tell you why something you said or did was hurtful. Listen to them, and make changes in the future. Don't try to tell them how you think they should feel.

Here are some steps you can take to avoid microaggressions.

How to Handle Microaggressions

If you're on the receiving end of a microaggression, it can be hard to make the other person understand why what they said or did upset you. Sometimes you might decide it isn't worth your time. You might feel like an argument would upset you even more. It's OK to pick your battles.

If you do want to speak up, you can ask the other person, "What did you mean by that?" You can also tell them politely but firmly, "I know you didn't mean to be rude, but what you just said was hurtful because … "

Facing the Facts

Talking to an adult or making friends who have experienced the same microaggressions can help people feel less alone. This can sometimes make microaggressions easier to deal with.

WHAT CAN YOU DO?

- Listen respectfully to people if they tell you that you said something hurtful.

- Talk to a trusted adult about your feelings.

- Read more about the things that make people different, such as race, gender, and religion.

- Think before you speak.

- Question your beliefs.

- Stand up for people when you hear microaggressions from others.

- Find friends who understand why microaggressions hurt.

Whether you've experienced microaggressions yourself or are trying to avoid hurting others, there are steps you can take.

GLOSSARY

accommodation: Something supplied that is useful and handy.
asexual: A person who is not physically attracted to other people.
compliment: Something nice said about someone. Or, to say nice things about someone.
depression: A mental illness with signs that include sadness, hopelessness, and a lack of interest in doing things that were once considered enjoyable.
discriminate: To treat people unequally based on class, race, religion, or another trait.
invalidate: To weaken or destroy the effect of something.
LGBTQ+ community: A group made up of people who see themselves as a gender different from the sex they were assigned at birth or who want to be in romantic relationships that aren't only male-female. LGBTQ stands for lesbian, gay, bisexual, transgender, and queer or questioning.
prejudice: An unfair feeling of dislike for a person or group because of race or religious or political beliefs, or another trait.
reinforce: To encourage or give support to an idea, feeling, or behavior.
segregation: A legal policy of keeping Black and white people separate.
sensitive: Easily harmed or damaged by certain conditions.
stereotype: A fixed idea that many people have about a thing or a group that is often untrue or only partly true.
transgender: Describing a person whose gender is different than the one they were assigned at birth.

FOR MORE INFORMATION

WEBSITES

Kiddle: Prejudice
kids.kiddle.co/Prejudice
Read more about prejudice here.

YouTube: Kids on Race
www.youtube.com/watch?v=C6xSyRJqle8
Listen to 12-year-olds explain how microaggressions make them feel.

BOOKS

Harris, Duchess, and Nadine Pinede. *Sexism and Race*. Minneapolis, MN: Essential Library, 2018.

Kaplan, Rebecca, and Avery Kaplan. *Double Challenge: Being LGBTQ and a Minority*. Philadelphia, PA: Mason Crest, 2020.

Kyi, Tanya Lloyd, and Drew Shannon. *This Is Your Brain on Stereotypes: How Science Is Tackling Unconscious Bias*. Toronto, ON: Kids Can Press, 2020.

Publisher's note to educators and parents: Our editors have carefully reviewed these websites to ensure that they are suitable for students. Many websites change frequently, however, and we cannot guarantee that a site's future contents will continue to meet our high standards of quality and educational value. Be advised that students should be closely supervised whenever they access the Internet.

INDEX

A
ableism, 12

D
depression, 16
disabilities, 6, 12

G
gender, 10, 14, 21

I
intersectionality, 14

L
LGBTQ+ community, 6, 10, 11

M
macroaggression, 5

P
Pierce, Chester M., 4
prejudice, 4, 6, 8, 10, 12, 14

R
racism, 8
religion, 7, 21

S
segregation, 5
stereotype, 18, 19

U
United States, 8

W
women, 6, 8, 14